- THE -
GARDEN
& THE &
CURTAIN
AND THE
CROSS

PACKED WITH PUZZLES, MAZES AND MORE!

Art and activity book

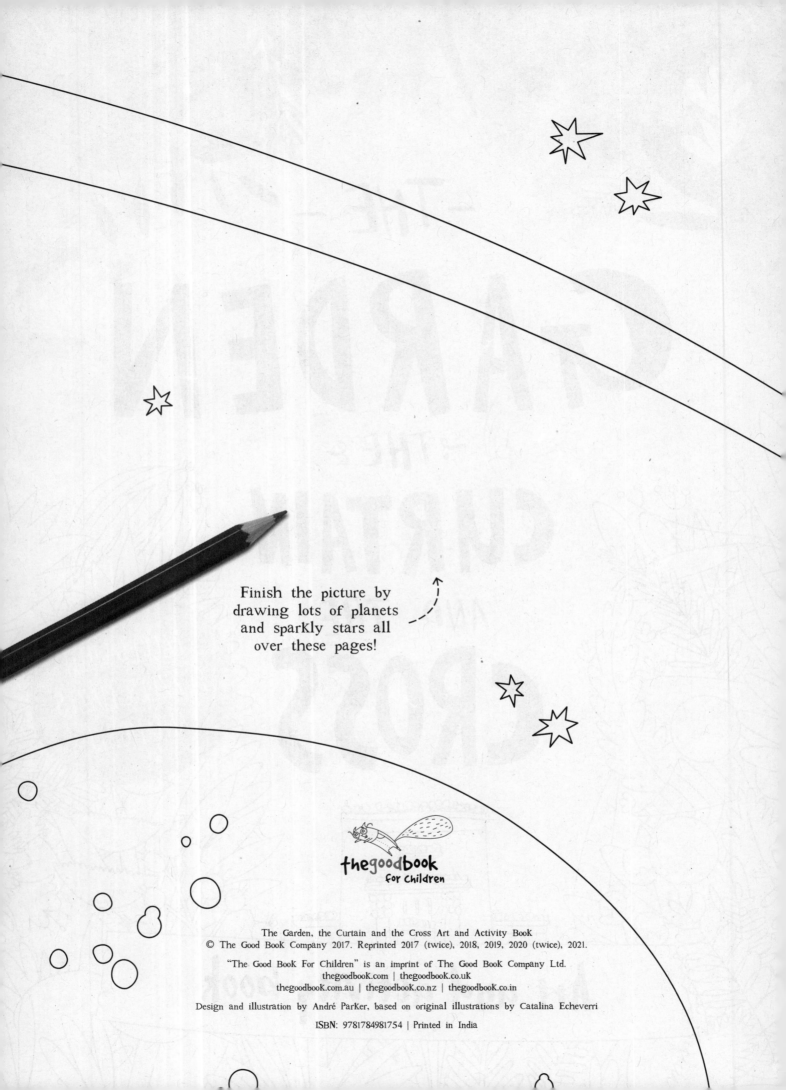

Finish the picture by
drawing lots of planets
and sparkly stars all
over these pages!

thegoodbook
for children

The Garden, the Curtain and the Cross Art and Activity Book
© The Good Book Company 2017. Reprinted 2017 (twice), 2018, 2019, 2020 (twice), 2021.

"The Good Book For Children" is an imprint of The Good Book Company Ltd.
thegoodbook.com | thegoodbook.co.uk
thegoodbook.com.au | thegoodbook.co.nz | thegoodbook.co.in

Design and illustration by André Parker, based on original illustrations by Catalina Echeverri

ISBN: 9781784981754 | Printed in India

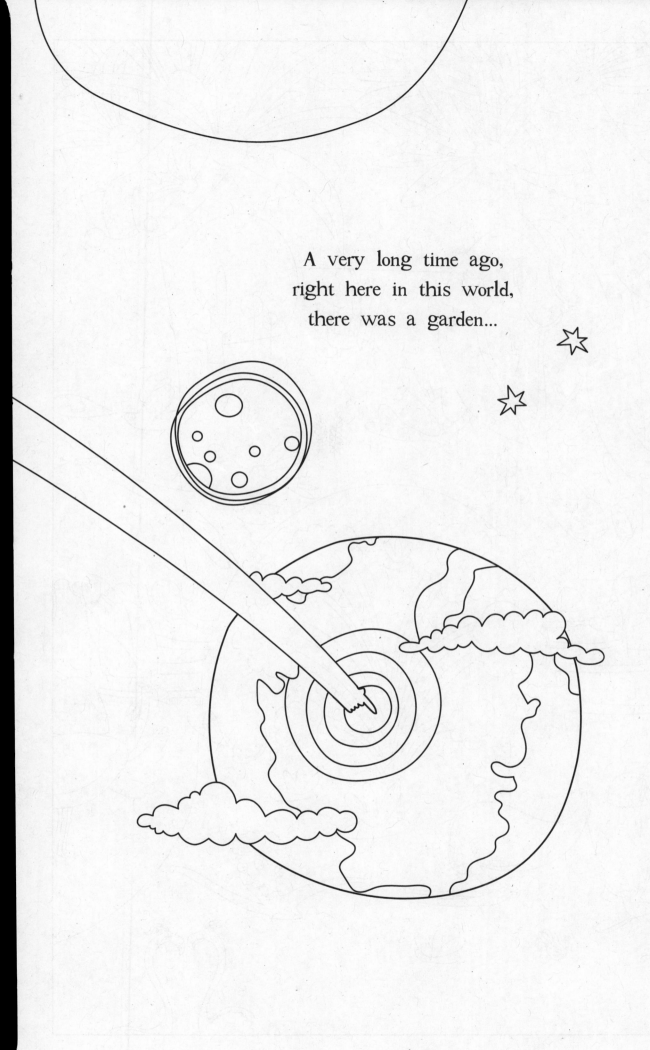

A very long time ago,
right here in this world,
there was a garden...

Match the shadows

God made all different kinds of
animals to live in his garden.
Can you help match them to their shadows?

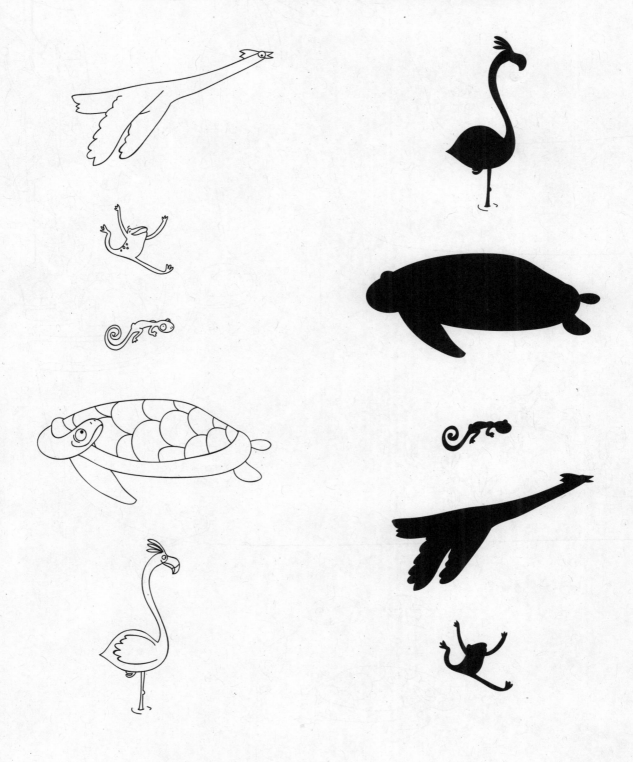

In the garden, everything was wonderful. The world was full of laughing and fun.

Fill the garden with plants, trees and animals - then decorate your picture!

Learn to draw

This animal is called a quagga. Follow the
steps to learn how to draw one...

Let's start with the
body, like this:

Next draw
this curve
for the mane

And add his head
and two ears

Now add a
swishy tail

And some
eyes

A few
stripes

And some
gallopy legs...
and you're
finished!

Draw one here running around in
God's wonderful garden!

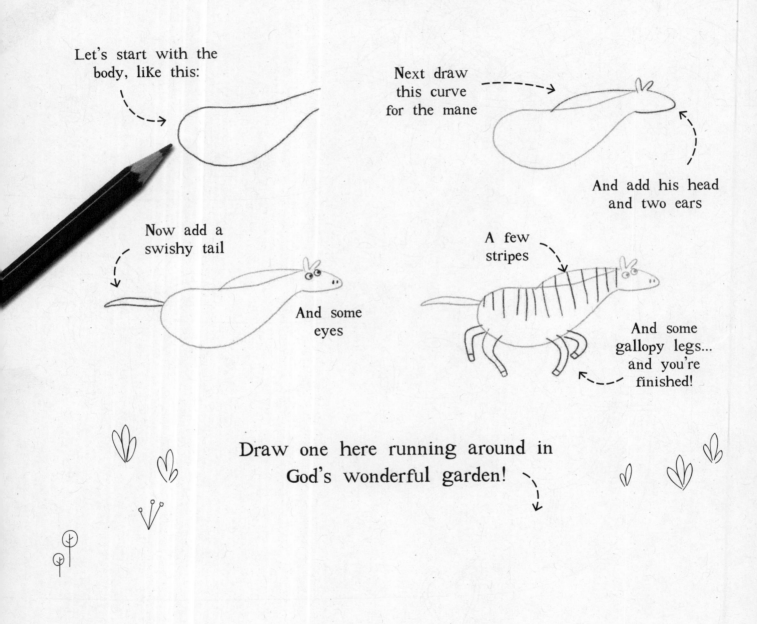

It was wonderful
to live with God.

But...

Sin

The people did a terrible thing.
They decided they didn't want God in charge.

God calls this "sin". Sin spoils things.
So sin has no place in God's wonderful garden...

The KEEP OUT maze

God sent the people outside.
He put warrior angels in front of the garden
like a big KEEP OUT sign.

b

a

Is there a way back
into the garden?

Wordsearch

h	K	i	g	b	h	r	g	s	y	s	a	j	h	u
n	e	l	f	r	u	i	t	r	z	a	n	e	r	y
e	K	i	j	u	f	t	r	h	b	r	i	v	e	r
u	v	r	m	a	g	t	e	s	l	k	m	d	n	v
y	h	e	d	e	s	r	s	b	g	a	a	o	a	t
h	e	o	i	n	a	e	n	a	d	l	l	v	n	b
p	g	z	s	a	K	e	z	o	o	r	s	u	g	K
y	o	i	i	b	d	p	i	g	l	y	i	r	e	a
l	K	h	u	r	o	p	e	l	e	K	i	d	l	w
a	l	x	a	w	o	u	t	s	i	d	e	c	u	n
z	j	g	f	p	s	u	f	s	z	t	b	m	h	o
s	i	o	p	h	p	b	w	r	h	f	a	d	a	m
e	t	r	b	m	l	y	r	g	j	t	i	c	i	n
t	o	g	e	t	h	e	r	l	y	u	f	g	i	l
s	u	e	g	t	e	y	m	v	e	x	i	s	f	a

☐ garden   ☐ tree   ☐ fruit

☐ animals   ☐ river   ☐ sin

☐ Adam   ☐ happy   ☐ outside

☐ Eve   ☐ together   ☐ angel

The KEEP OUT curtain

God told the people to build a special building where he would live. Then he told them to put a big curtain around this wonderful place.

Use lots of blue, red, purple and gold!

Decorate the curtain with lots of angels and patterns.

Time passes...

Hundreds of years passed by, and the KEEP OUT curtain stayed in the temple.

Finish the picture by drawing lots of men, women, boys and girls on the family tree - then decorate your picture!

Then, one day, God's Son came to live in this world as a person.

He was called...

Jesus!

Jesus always did what God said. Jesus never sinned.

Jesus visited the temple where the
KEEP OUT curtain hung.

Can you decorate
the temple?

Jesus said that God had sent him
to open the way back to God's
wonderful place. But...

The cross

People still didn't want God in charge. They put Jesus on a cross to die. It was the most bad thing that had ever happened. BUT...

On the cross, Jesus took our sin. All the bad things we do, and all the sad things they cause - Jesus took them all!

Write or draw on the cross all the bad things we do. Jesus has taken them all!

Trace over the dotted line to make a great big tear!

The curtain tore!

When Jesus died, God ripped up
the KEEP OUT sign!

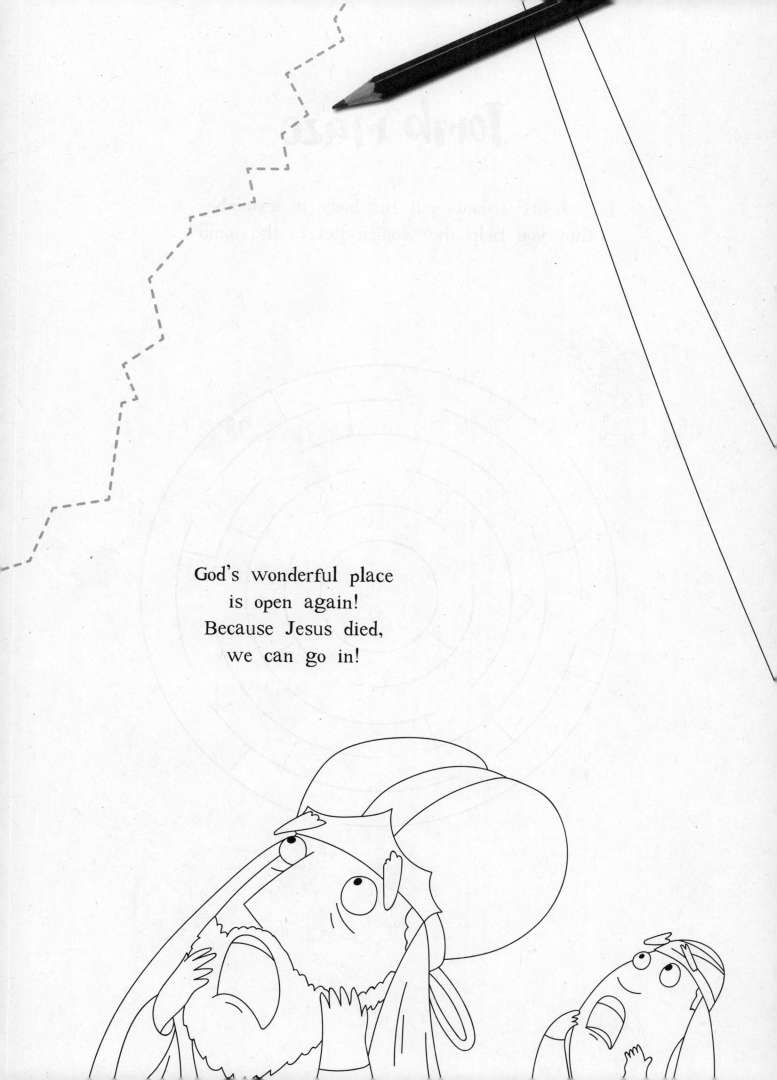

God's wonderful place
is open again!
Because Jesus died,
we can go in!

Tomb maze

Jesus' friends put his body in a tomb.
Can you help the women get to the tomb?

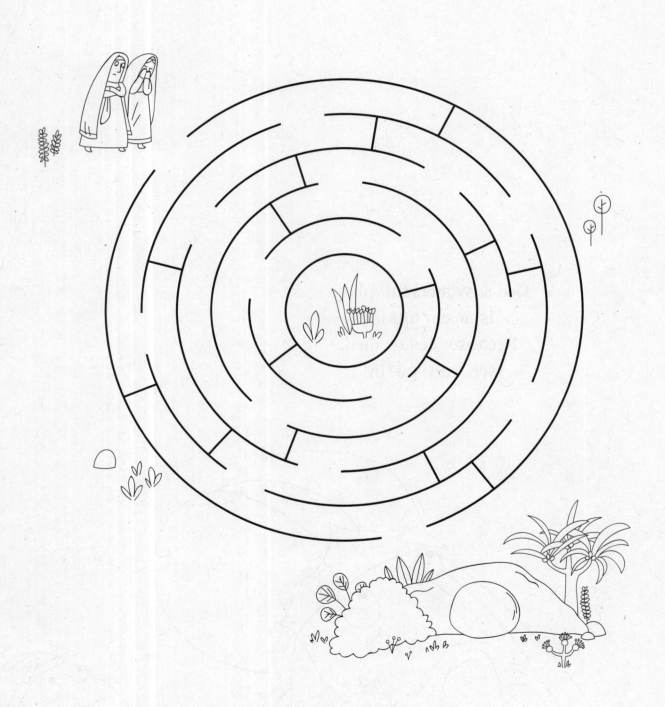

Alive again!

God brought Jesus back to life so that he could live in God's wonderful place for ever!

Decorate this picture of Jesus
with all his happy friends!

Jesus has sent us all an invitation to come
and live with him there too!

Decorate Jesus'
cloak with lots
of patterns

How about some
more swirly curls
on this tunic?

Wordsearch

h	a	l	i	v	e	r	g	s	y	s	a	j	h	u
c	h	l	s	r	g	i	s	r	z	a	k	e	s	y
r	k	a	j	u	e	t	r	a	b	b	e	v	p	m
o	w	r	r	t	g	t	e	s	r	l	f	d	e	v
s	h	e	i	a	p	b	o	b	p	a	a	o	c	t
s	e	v	i	n	s	e	k	m	d	l	h	p	i	b
p	n	z	c	a	k	i	e	o	b	r	s	e	a	k
i	o	i	i	u	d	t	i	g	l	y	i	n	l	a
l	k	h	u	a	r	p	e	l	e	k	i	d	t	w
a	l	x	r	w	x	t	f	s	i	s	u	c	u	n
z	j	h	f	p	s	b	a	b	y	t	a	m	h	o
s	i	o	p	h	g	b	w	i	h	f	o	r	n	p
j	e	s	u	s	l	y	r	g	n	t	i	c	a	n
t	e	f	r	i	e	n	d	s	y	u	f	g	c	h
s	u	e	g	t	e	y	m	f	o	r	e	v	e	r

☐ temple   ☐ baby   ☐ alive

☐ curtain   ☐ cross   ☐ open

☐ special   ☐ tomb   ☐ invite

☐ Jesus   ☐ friends   ☐ forever

Join the dots

Start at 1 and draw a line to each dot to discover what Jesus is sitting on...

Now decorate your picture!

We can live with God for ever!
There will be nothing bad, and no one sad.

Draw some happy and smiling faces on
these people!

Living with God

Can you complete this picture?
Draw lots of animals, trees, flowers
and happy, happy people!

Draw a shining
city on this hill

Here's a space
for all the happy
people!

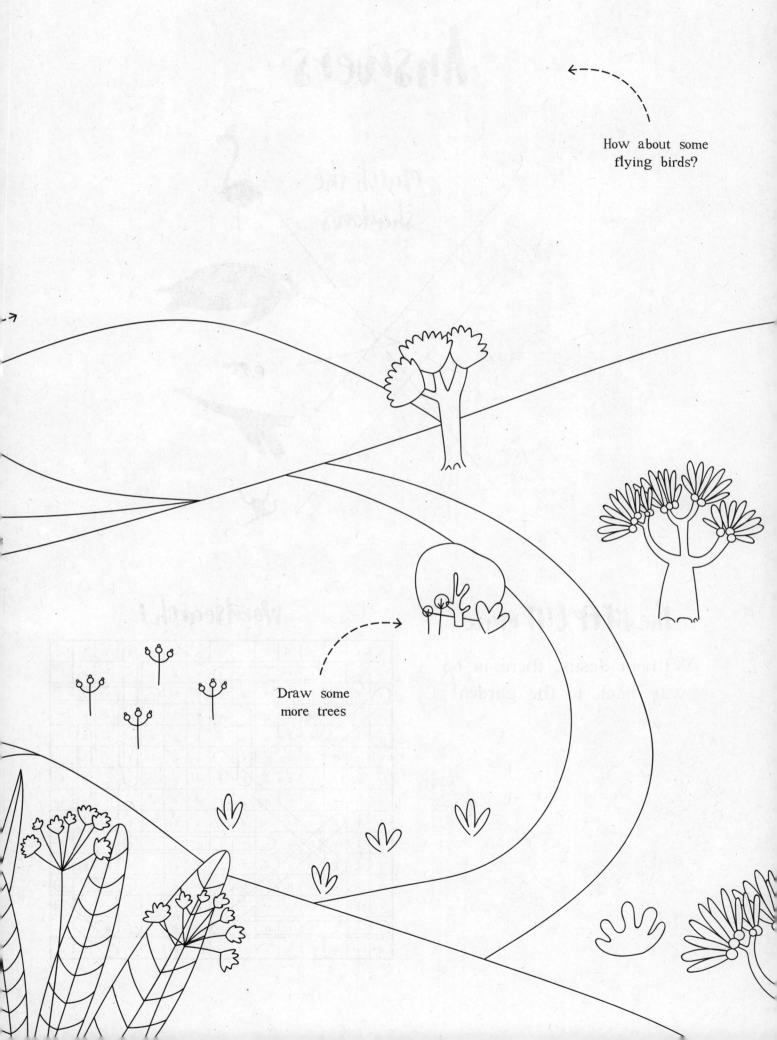

How about some flying birds?

Draw some more trees

Answers

Match the shadows

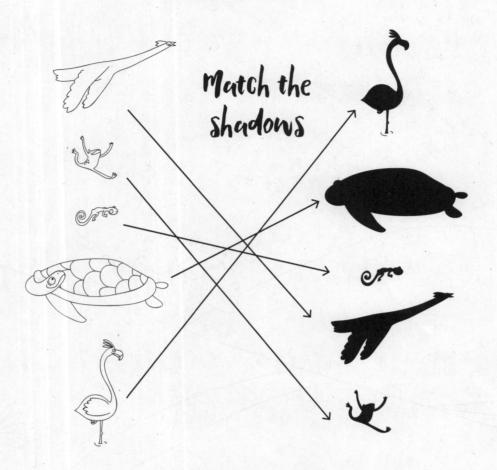

The KEEP OUT maze

Without Jesus, there is no way back to the garden!

Wordsearch 1

h	k	i	g	b	h	r	g	s	y	s	a	j	h	u
n	e	l	f	r	u	i	t	r	z	a	n	e	r	y
e	k	i	j	u	f	t	r	h	b	r	i	v	e	r
u	v	r	m	a	g	t	e	s	l	k	m	d	n	v
y	h	e	d	e	s	r	s	b	g	a	a	o	a	t
h	e	o	i	n	a	e	n	a	d	l	l	v	n	b
p	g	z	s	a	k	e	z	o	o	r	s	u	g	k
y	o	i	i	b	d	p	i	g	l	y	i	r	e	a
l	k	h	u	r	o	p	e	l	e	k	i	d	l	w
a	l	x	a	w	o	u	t	s	i	d	e	c	u	n
z	j	g	f	p	s	u	f	s	z	t	b	m	h	o
s	i	o	p	h	p	b	w	r	h	f	a	d	a	m
e	t	r	b	m	l	y	r	g	j	t	i	c	i	n
t	o	g	e	t	h	e	r	l	y	u	f	g	i	l
s	u	e	g	t	e	y	m	v	e	x	i	s	f	a

Tomb maze

Join the dots

It's a horse!

Wordsearch 2

h	a	l	i	v	e	r	g	s	y	s	a	j	h	u
c	h	l	s	r	g	i	s	r	z	a	k	e	s	y
r	k	a	j	u	e	t	r	a	b	b	e	v	p	m
o	w	r	r	t	g	t	e	s	r	l	f	d	e	v
s	h	e	i	a	p	b	o	b	p	a	a	o	c	t
s	e	v	i	n	s	e	k	m	d	l	h	p	i	b
p	n	z	c	a	k	i	e	o	b	r	s	e	a	K
i	o	i	i	u	d	t	i	g	l	y	i	n	l	a
l	k	h	u	a	r	p	e	l	e	k	i	d	t	w
a	l	x	r	w	x	t	f	s	i	s	u	c	u	n
z	j	h	f	p	s	b	a	b	y	t	a	m	h	o
s	i	o	p	h	g	b	w	i	h	f	o	r	n	p
j	e	s	u	s	l	y	r	g	n	t	i	c	a	n
t	e	f	r	i	e	n	d	s	y	u	f	g	c	h
s	u	e	g	t	e	y	m	f	o	r	e	v	e	r

Now read the book!

If you enjoyed this activity book, read the full story in 'The Garden, the Curtain and the Cross.'

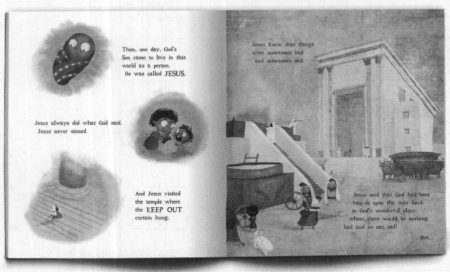

Other books available in the award-winning "Tales That Tell The Truth" series: